# ECONOMICS OF ENTERTAINMENT

# THE ECONOMICS OF A ROCK CONCERT

Sheri Perl

## Crabtree Publishing Company
www.crabtreebooks.com

**Author:** Sheri Perl
**Editor-in-chief:** Lionel Bender
**Editors:** Simon Adams, Rachel Eagen
**Proofreaders:** Laura Booth, Wendy Scavuzzo
**Project coordinator:** Kathy Middleton
**Design and photo research:** Ben White
**Cover design:** Margaret Amy Salter
**Production:** Kim Richardson
**Print and production coordinator:**
    Margaret Amy Salter
**Prepress technician:** Margaret Amy Salter

**Consultant:** Laura Ebert, Ph.D., Lecturer in
Economics at the State University of New
York at New Paltz, N.Y.

This book was produced for
Crabtree Publishing Company by
Bender Richardson White.

**Photographs and reproductions:**
Getty Images: 14–15 (Digital Vision), 22–23 (AFP), 26–27 (AFP),
28–29 (Rick Diamond), 32–33 (Bryan Bedder). Shutterstock.com:
cover-top (dwphotos), cover-center (Keith Tarrier), cover-top right
insets (Sergii Korolko), cover-bottom right inset (Susan Quinland-
Stringer), cover-bottom left inset (Alexey Laputin), banners (Goran
Djukanovic), icons (Semisatch, Warren Goldswain, Viorel Sima,
Piotr Marcinski, Dario Sabljak, optimarc, Alexander Demyanenko),
1 bottom middle (Randy Miramontez), 4-5 (Randy Miramontez), 6-
7 (Bojana Ristic), 8-9 (Goran Djukanovic), 10–11 (Anibal Trejo),
12–13 (Erika Cross), 15 top right (Miguel Campos), 16–17 (Tsian),
18–19 (Dmitrydesign), 19 top right (TDC Photography), 20–21
(CyberEak), 24–25 (antb), 28 middle
(Foto-Ruhrgebiet), 30–31 (Andreas Gradin), 31 middle right
(jumpingsack), 34–35 (Christian Bertrand), 36–37 (Dusan Jankovic),
38 middle left (Peshkov Daniil), 38–39 (glen Gaffney), 40 middle left
(Darko Zeljkovic), 40–41, 42–43 top (Christian Bertrand), 42–43.
NFL, Live Nation, Generation Records, Pepsi, Arm & Hammer and
other manufacturers and brands are registered trademarks and/or
are protected by copyright. They are usually given with a ™, ®,
or © symbol.

**Graphics:** Stefan Chabluk

**Library and Archives Canada Cataloguing in Publication**

Perl, Sheri, author
    The economics of a rock concert / Sheri Perl.

(Economics of entertainment)
Includes index.
Issued in print and electronic formats.
ISBN 978-0-7787-7969-8 (bound).--ISBN 978-0-7787-7974-2 (pbk.).--
ISBN 978-1-4271-7868-8 (pdf).--ISBN 978-1-4271-7983-8 (html)

    1. Rock music--Economic aspects--Juvenile literature. 2. Rock
concerts--Production and direction--Juvenile literature. 3. Music
trade--Juvenile literature. I. Title.

ML3790.P452 2014          j781.66          C2013-907575-5
                                           C2013-907576-3

**Library of Congress Cataloging-in-Publication Data**

Perl, Sheri, 1967-, author.
    The economics of a rock concert / Sheri Perl.
        pages cm. -- (Economics of entertainment)
    Includes index.
    ISBN 978-0-7787-7969-8 (reinforced library binding) -- ISBN
978-0-7787-7974-2 (pbk.) -- ISBN 978-1-4271-7868-8 (electronic
pdf) -- ISBN 978-1-4271-7983-8 (electronic html)
    1. Rock concerts--Economic aspects--Juvenile literature.
2. Music trade--Juvenile literature. I. Title.

ML3790.P43 2014
781.66068--dc23

                                    2013043400

# Crabtree Publishing Company

www.crabtreebooks.com          1-800-387-7650

Printed in Canada/022014/MA20131220

**Published in Canada**
**Crabtree Publishing**
616 Welland Ave.
St. Catharines, ON
L2M 5V6

**Published in the United States**
**Crabtree Publishing**
PMB 59051
350 Fifth Avenue, 59th Floor
New York, New York 10118

**Published in the United Kingdom**
**Crabtree Publishing**
Maritime House
Basin Road North, Hove
BN41 1WR

**Published in Australia**
**Crabtree Publishing**
3 Charles Street
Coburg North
VIC, 3058

# CONTENTS

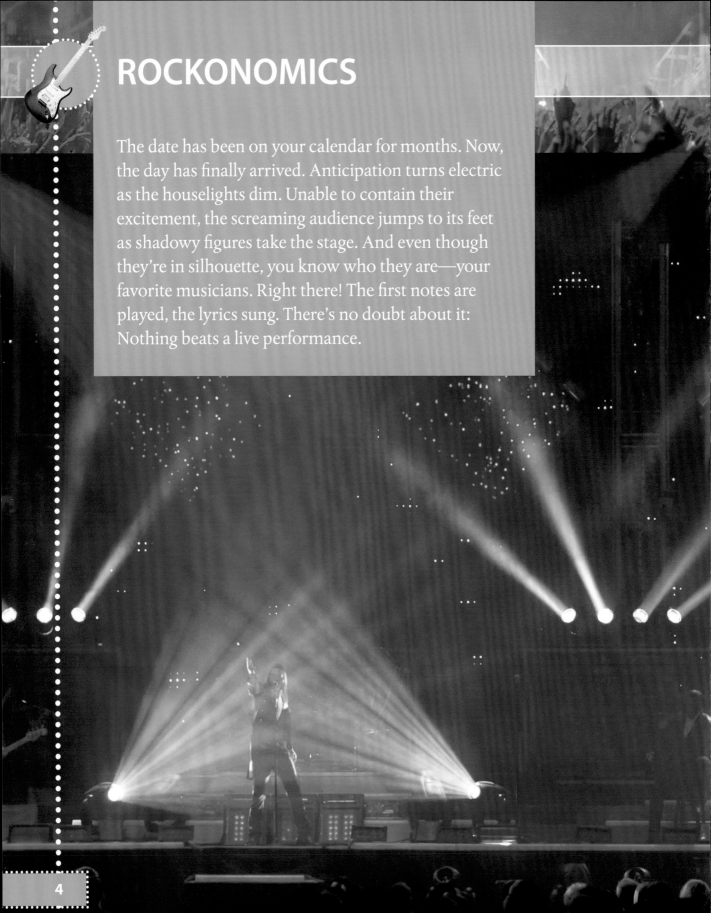

# ROCKONOMICS

The date has been on your calendar for months. Now, the day has finally arrived. Anticipation turns electric as the houselights dim. Unable to contain their excitement, the screaming audience jumps to its feet as shadowy figures take the stage. And even though they're in silhouette, you know who they are—your favorite musicians. Right there! The first notes are played, the lyrics sung. There's no doubt about it: Nothing beats a live performance.

The Trans-Siberian Orchestra performs at the Power Balance Pavilion (now Sleep Train Arena) in Sacramento, California, on November 19, 2011.

## TICKETS, PLEASE!

Did you ever stop to wonder what made this concert possible? Who were the key players? What was needed to bring it from concept to concert? Who decided how much to charge for the tickets? Where does all the money from ticket sales and other **revenue streams** go? The discipline of **economics** can help you answer all of these questions. Economics deals with the **production** (putting on a concert), **distribution** (ticket sales), and consumption (by you) of goods and services (the concert).

## WHAT DO YOU THINK?

First, consider your **cash flow** (money in and out) and monthly **fixed expenses** and **varied expenses**. With your **limited resources**, deciding between the things you need (food) and the things you want (a concert ticket) is sometimes tricky. Looking at the figures on the right, how many months will it take Liam to save for a ticket?

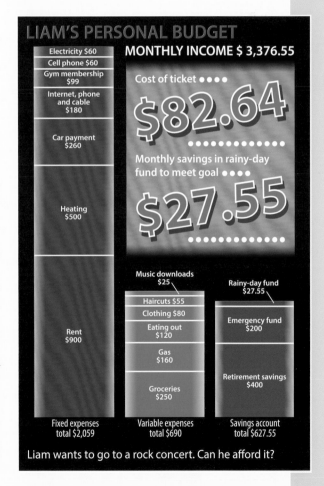

LIAM'S PERSONAL BUDGET

**MONTHLY INCOME $ 3,376.55**

Electricity $60
Cell phone $60
Gym membership $99
Internet, phone and cable $180
Car payment $260
Heating $500
Rent $900

Cost of ticket ●●●●
**$82.64**
Monthly savings in rainy-day fund to meet goal ●●●●
**$27.55**

Music downloads $25
Haircuts $55
Clothing $80
Eating out $120
Gas $160
Groceries $250

Rainy-day fund $27.55
Emergency fund $200
Retirement savings $400

Fixed expenses total $2,059

Variable expenses total $690

Savings account total $627.55

Liam wants to go to a rock concert. Can he afford it?

# A MUSICAL IDEA!

## FROM SMALL BEGINNINGS

It all starts with an idea. Someone at sometime said, "I bet I can make money by charging admission to hear musicians perform live." And they were correct! The concert industry has become a multi-billion dollar business. Today, this person in the concert industry is called the promoter. The promoter thinks of a band he or she wants to promote or present to the audience. Then he or she considers if the band can fill a stadium or a smaller venue (the facility where the concert will be held). Is it going to be a single-act show or a multi-act music festival?

### WHAT DO YOU THINK?

Do you like coming up with brand new ideas that no one has thought of before? If so, then you just may grow up to be an **entrepreneur**. An entrepreneur is a person who comes up with money-making ideas. Imagine being the first person to come up with the concept of rock concerts.

## IT HAD TO START SOMEWHERE

Many people believe the first live rock concert ever was the Moondog Coronation Ball in Cleveland, Ohio, on March 21, 1952. Alan Freed, or Moondog, a radio announcer, unknowingly became the first rock 'n' roll promoter, and as such is referred to as "the Father of Rock 'n' Roll." He knew how popular rhythm 'n' blues—the grandfather of rock 'n' roll—was among teenagers at the time. Freed thought he would sell tickets to an event featuring some of these artists for a live performance. Tickets were $1.50 in advance, or $1.75 at the door. Teens lined up eagerly and seats were sold out in minutes. Today, anyone looking in on this scene would view this as normal concert behavior. But at the time no one had ever even heard the phrase "rock concert." When about 25,000 fans showed up at the venue, which seated only 10,000, Freed knew he had stumbled upon a brand new market—the concert industry.

Due to supply and demand, tickets for a major rock concert—for maybe 20,000 seats—can sell out in less than 60 seconds. Amazing!

## CONCERT TOURS

The 1960s marked the true beginning of concert tours. At first, however, most bands made their living predominately from record sales, not concerts. And, because of this, concert tickets were much cheaper than now. As the age of the Internet flourished and downloading music became wildly popular, the loss of profit for record sales reached an all-time low. The music industry had to revamp their ideas. Large-venue world tours became the new way artists made money. This change in the industry was brought on by you, the **consumer**. While the demand for records decreased and the demand for concert tickets increased, the cost for records dwindled while concert ticket prices sky-rocketed. This is called **supply and demand**.

### TOP TEN BIGGEST CONCERTS OF ALL TIME

| | | |
|---|---|---|
| 1 | 1994 | Rod Stewart at the Copa – 3,500,000 |
| 2 | 1986 | N.Y.C. Philharmonic in Central Park – 800,000 |
| 3 | 1997 | Garth Brooks in Central Park – 750,000 |
| 4 | 1983 | Steve Wozniak's U.S. Festival – 670,000 |
| 5 | 1973 | Summer Jam at Watkins Glen – 600,000 plus |
| 6 | 1970 | Isle of Wight Festival – 600,000 |
| 7 | 1981 | Simon and Garfunkel Reunion – 500,000 |
| 8 | 2003 | Toronto SARS Benefit – 450,000 plus |
| 9 | 1969 | Woodstock – 400,000 |
| 10 | 1997 | Blockbuster RockFest – 385,000 |

Who has played to the most people in music history.

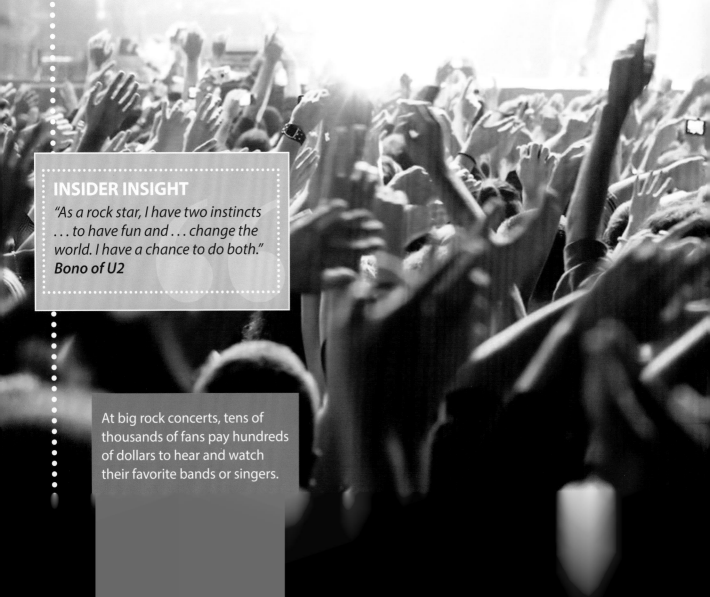

# 1 THE CONCERT INDUSTRY

Imagine you are a concert promoter. You love your job. It's fast-paced and ever-changing. You get to meet all types of exciting people, not only musicians, but all the people involved in putting on a concert. You and other key players in the music industry influence the global **economy**. But the greatest impact on a band's success is the consumer.

## INSIDER INSIGHT

*"As a rock star, I have two instincts . . . to have fun and . . . change the world. I have a chance to do both."*
***Bono of U2***

At big rock concerts, tens of thousands of fans pay hundreds of dollars to hear and watch their favorite bands or singers.

## A PIECE OF THE PIE

It takes hundreds of paid professionals to put on a rock concert. Some are paid a salary (weekly, monthly, or any regular income), while others are paid **commission** (a percentage from the **profit**). The profit is what's left over after you subtract the costs from the ticket sales and other revenue.

As the promoter, you earn perhaps 15 percent of the profit. But, before you make any money, you'll need to pay the venue upfront. Therefore, as a promoter, you begin at a loss of profit and hope you will not only **recoup** that money but make a profit. The venue will make 100 percent from all parking fees and, depending on the artist, 15 percent of all merchandise such as T-shirts and posters. What about the artist? Before they can make any money, they have a staff to pay!

### WHAT DO YOU THINK?

Would you rather be paid a set salary, like the touring manager, or make a commission from the profits, like the artist's manager? Why?

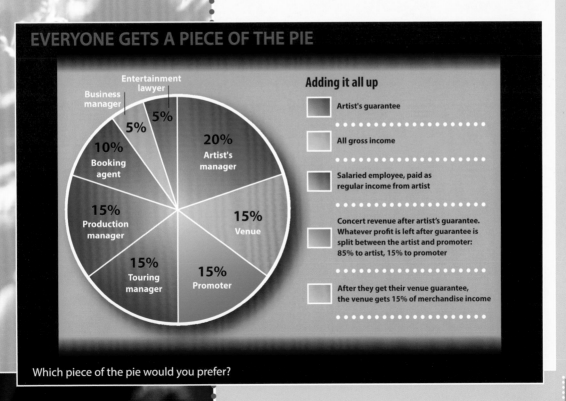

## EVERYONE GETS A PIECE OF THE PIE

Pie chart:
- 20% Artist's manager
- 15% Venue
- 15% Promoter
- 15% Touring manager
- 15% Production manager
- 10% Booking agent
- 5% Business manager
- 5% Entertainment lawyer

### Adding it all up

- **Artist's guarantee**
- **All gross income**
- **Salaried employee, paid as regular income from artist**
- **Concert revenue after artist's guarantee. Whatever profit is left after guarantee is split between the artist and promoter: 85% to artist, 15% to promoter**
- **After they get their venue guarantee, the venue gets 15% of merchandise income**

Which piece of the pie would you prefer?

## SUPPLY AND DEMAND

A concert is an **experience good**, a product you pay for before knowing its quality. The desire to hear musicians perform live is so strong that fans will pay almost anything. The concert industry is the only form of entertainment untouched by the recent economic **recession** (a period of high unemployment and failing businesses). Some goods will experience **deflation** (a decrease in the cost of goods) during a recession. However, concert tickets continue to experience **inflation** (the rising cost of goods). When a concert is sold out, there are not enough tickets to feed the demand of the fans. This is called **scarcity**. Devoted fans create such a fever that tickets become a hot commodity—a good with such appeal that the supply of the good cannot satisfy the demand, in turn driving the price of tickets up.

This is why concert tickets are so expensive. To purchase them, you will have to consider the **opportunity cost** and the **trade-off** you'll need to make. The trade-off is what you're willing to sacrifice in order to afford the tickets. Say you're willing to skip seeing seven movies to have the money to pay for your tickets. The trade-off is the movies for the concert tickets. The opportunity cost of the tickets is the dollar value of what you could have chosen to spend your money on instead of buying the tickets.

Our economic system is called the **free market**. The free market allows businesses, instead of the government, to set their own prices. Free markets allow people to make choices about their own spending.

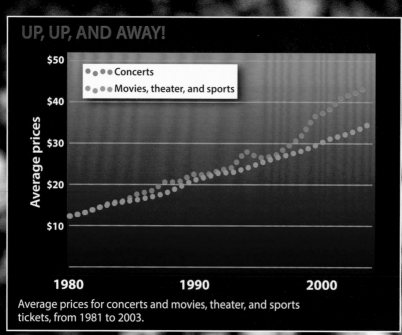

### UP, UP, AND AWAY!

- ●●● Concerts
- ●●● Movies, theater, and sports

Average prices for concerts and movies, theater, and sports tickets, from 1981 to 2003.

Samuel Titos, member of Dover, performs to large crowds in Barcelona, Spain, on September 22, 2012.

**WHAT DO YOU THINK?**

Put these examples of goods in order, from most likely to least likely to meet the demand of consumers: an Apple iPad, tickets to see an NFL game, clothing, tickets to see Justin Timberlake, food, and tickets to a Broadway show. Besides the Justin Timberlake tickets, which of these is most like the concert industry?

# 2 FROM CONCEPT TO CONCERT

No matter the size of the fan base or the popularity of an artist, all concerts begin with the same three components: talent, venue, and **marketing**. To choose the appropriately sized venue, a promoter must consider the talent, or artist, and his or her popularity. If you predict the artist can sell out the venue, then you have a match and can move forward with an offer to the talent's agent. Only then will you begin the last step, which is marketing or advertising the concert.

Madison Square Garden is home to the NY Knicks, NY Rangers, and NY Liberty, but it is also one of the largest indoor concert arenas in the world.

## THE RECORD BREAKERS

Live Nation Entertainment is the largest producer and promoter of live music events in the world (according to Live Nation). Live Nation owns and operates 84 venues. If you've seen a concert, chances are you saw it in a venue owned by Live Nation.

## IT'S AS EASY AS ONE, TWO, THREE: STEP ONE—THE TALENT

First up is to identify the talent you want to promote. If it's BIG talent, such as One Direction or Bruno Mars, then you will likely be able to fill a large stadium and your show will sell out in record time. However, lesser-known artists, such as Alt-J or Vampire Weekend, may not have the same draw . . . yet! After all, not everyone can sell out Madison Square Garden. The name of the game is to make a profit. For that reason, a promoter must always think in terms of how many seats will sell.

Say you book a large venue of 20,000 seats with an unknown artist. Most likely, he or she will be unable to fill those seats and you will take a hit or suffer a loss of profit. A loss of profit is when the cost is more than the revenue (the money made before costs are subtracted) and you are in the **negative numbers**! That's very bad.

Think: Big names = big venues; lesser known artists = smaller concert halls. Here's another way to think about it: The more seats sold, the more revenue generated, therefore, the more profit earned. For that reason, fitting the right artist to the correct-sized venue is vital, not only to your success as a promoter but to your hard-earned reputation of knowing your industry well and your ability to correctly judge a talent's appeal!

## STEP TWO—THE VENUE

The next step is to put the venue on hold. Then, contact the talent's agent, tell them your vision, that you have the venue on hold, and make your offer. If the artist is going on a world tour, many promoters from all over the world will also be contacting the agent. Likewise, the artist will have several agents specializing in specific territories. Some artists have touring managers who keep the world tour well organized. All of these people—the various promoters, touring managers, and agents—work together to create the itinerary for the tour. Once all of them agree to the terms, each promoter will pay rent to their selected venue. The promoter then prepares a **budget**, projecting costs, sales, and profits. The promoter will also hire people to perfect sound, lighting, and other technical aspects. Catering and security crews are also hired. When the artist agrees to the terms, you can then move on to the final step.

## STEP THREE—MARKETING

Marketing, or promoting, the concert is the final step. The goal of promotion is to excite fans about the concert tour. There are many ways this can be done, such as through print ads, newspapers, flyers, and billboards. Radio announcements account for a large percentage of concert promotion. But the most effective marketing tool today is social media such as Facebook, Twitter, and Instagram. Most artists have their own Twitter accounts. Talent . . . check! Venue . . . check! Marketing . . . check!

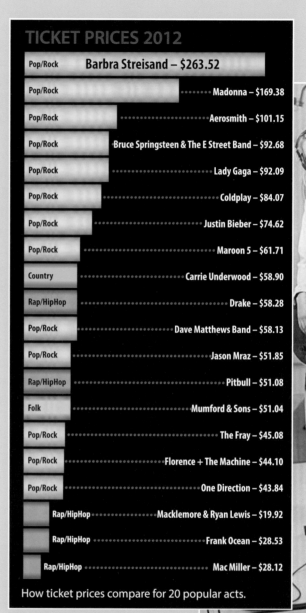

**TICKET PRICES 2012**

|  |  |
|---|---|
| Pop/Rock | Barbra Streisand – $263.52 |
| Pop/Rock | Madonna – $169.38 |
| Pop/Rock | Aerosmith – $101.15 |
| Pop/Rock | Bruce Springsteen & The E Street Band – $92.68 |
| Pop/Rock | Lady Gaga – $92.09 |
| Pop/Rock | Coldplay – $84.07 |
| Pop/Rock | Justin Bieber – $74.62 |
| Pop/Rock | Maroon 5 – $61.71 |
| Country | Carrie Underwood – $58.90 |
| Rap/HipHop | Drake – $58.28 |
| Pop/Rock | Dave Matthews Band – $58.13 |
| Pop/Rock | Jason Mraz – $51.85 |
| Rap/HipHop | Pitbull – $51.08 |
| Folk | Mumford & Sons – $51.04 |
| Pop/Rock | The Fray – $45.08 |
| Pop/Rock | Florence + The Machine – $44.10 |
| Pop/Rock | One Direction – $43.84 |
| Rap/HipHop | Macklemore & Ryan Lewis – $19.92 |
| Rap/HipHop | Frank Ocean – $28.53 |
| Rap/HipHop | Mac Miller – $28.12 |

How ticket prices compare for 20 popular acts.

There are many people who work behind the scenes to get music out into the world. Here, a music producer adjusts the sound mixer during a recording session.

## THE RECORD BREAKERS

- Over 30 percent of teens in the U.S.A. attended a concert in 2012
- 85 percent of adults listen to music an average of 3.5 hours every day
- 58 percent of Americans say music is an integral part of their lives
- 60 percent of concert goers are likely to purchase a product from a sponsor

It's all part of the big picture! Signing autographs for eager fans, singer Enrique Bunbury promotes his new album in Mexico City, Mexico, in 2010.

# TO MARKET, TO MARKET

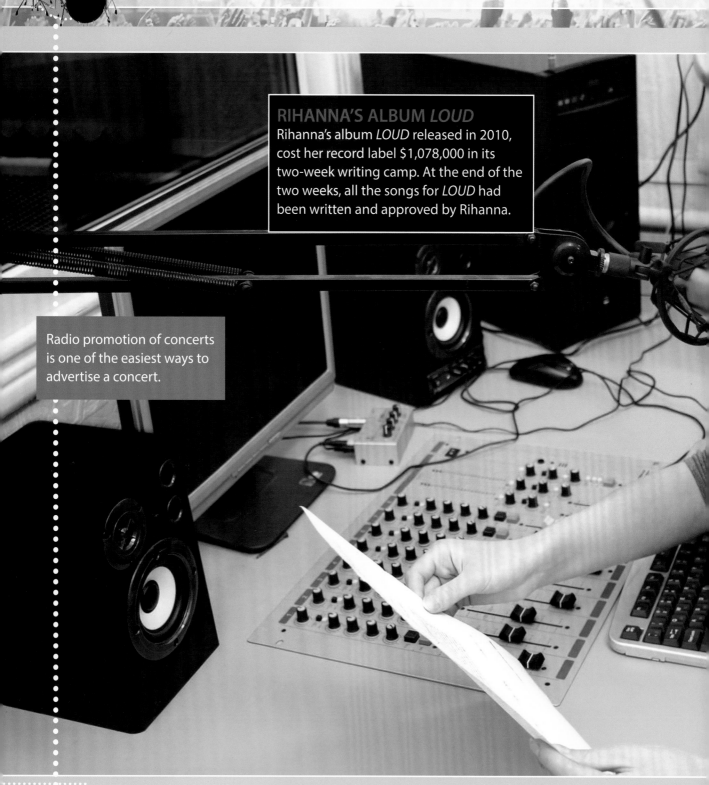

**RIHANNA'S ALBUM *LOUD***
Rihanna's album *LOUD* released in 2010, cost her record label $1,078,000 in its two-week writing camp. At the end of the two weeks, all the songs for *LOUD* had been written and approved by Rihanna.

Radio promotion of concerts is one of the easiest ways to advertise a concert.

## MARKETING

Marketing is more than just radio announcements and tweets. Television interviews are another way to promote music. Fans love to see the personalities of their favorite artists. They love to know the story behind the public persona they portray. Another marketing tool is autographs. Often, music stores, such as Generation Records in New York City, will hold artist signings, where fans line up with something for an artist to sign such as a poster or T-shirt. It's that chance to get close to a star.

## WRITING CAMP

Musicians, such as the Eagles or Paul McCartney, have proven track records of producing hit after hit. Their name alone is enough to draw sold-out audiences to their concerts without needing to produce any new music. But for today's newer musicians, such as Rihanna, it is necessary for them to first produce a new album with at least one hit song. These artists need a hit song that saturates the radio. A musician's record label, manager, and agent sometimes spend close to $1 million to create a hit song. One way to do this is through a writing camp. Writing camp is an opportunity for an artist's team to hire the best songwriters and musicians from all over the world to come together for two solid weeks of songwriting. At the end of those two weeks, the artist will approve every song that will appear on their next album. Anticipation rises as the waiting game begins. Will any of the songs be a hit? If so, the **investment** was worthwhile.

### WHAT DO YOU THINK?

Economists say you have to spend money to make money. This seems to be what the music industry believes. Can you think of a time in your life when you may be willing to take such a risk?

17

# IT'S SHOWTIME!

## ON THE ROAD

Before you know it, it's time to take the whole show on the road. This is the moment when your concept turns into an actual concert. Remember that production is the making of goods and services. Production is involved in creating an album and making merchandise to sell. But the biggest part of producing a rock concert is the concert itself!

One of the most complex tasks in producing a concert is building the stage. Modern stages can be quite elaborate, with multi-levels and cranes that lift singers up and over the audience while rotating nearly 360 degrees. Many shows feature huge LED (light-emitting diode) screens, pyrotechnics, fog machines, lasers, and confetti airbursts that rain down confetti from up above the audience. All of these special effects create jobs for roadies, or skilled laborers.

For large acts such as Aerosmith it can take as many as 200 roadies to produce a concert. About 20 semi-trucks will arrive on the scene with the band's equipment and begin unloading and setting everything up. About 100 miles (161 km) of electric cable will need to be unraveled and more than 600 lights will need to be hung. It takes as much electricity to put on a rock concert as to power a 25-story building! It begins at 8 A.M. and, in as little as 12 hours, the arena is ready to go. At the end of the night, the roadies will tear it all down. What took 12 hours to set up takes about 2.5 hours to pack away. Then it's on to the next city!

Because of the **human resources** (skilled laborers) needed to produce a concert, concerts feed the job market and fuel the economy. So, the next time you buy a concert ticket, you can feel good knowing that you've just created jobs for many people.

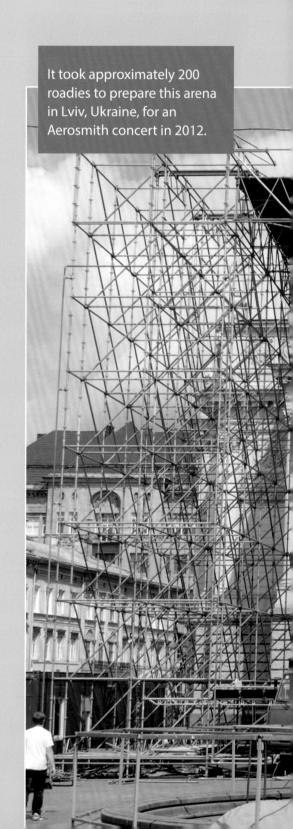

It took approximately 200 roadies to prepare this arena in Lviv, Ukraine, for an Aerosmith concert in 2012.

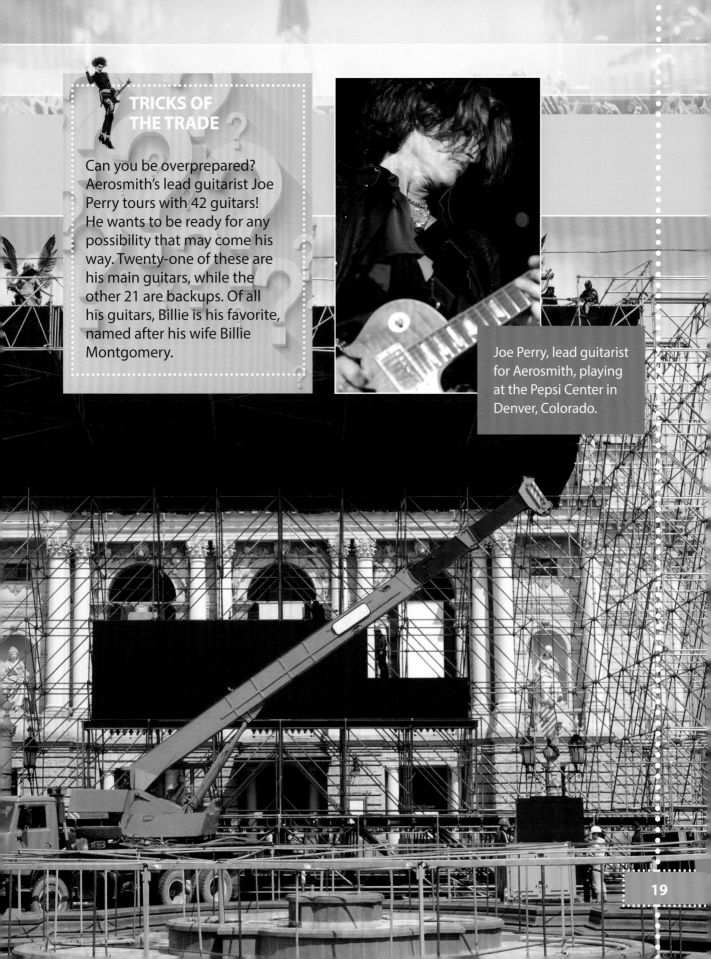

## TRICKS OF THE TRADE

Can you be overprepared? Aerosmith's lead guitarist Joe Perry tours with 42 guitars! He wants to be ready for any possibility that may come his way. Twenty-one of these are his main guitars, while the other 21 are backups. Of all his guitars, Billie is his favorite, named after his wife Billie Montgomery.

Joe Perry, lead guitarist for Aerosmith, playing at the Pepsi Center in Denver, Colorado.

# 3 WHO'S RESPONSIBLE?

Before a profit can be made, a few items need to be settled or reconciled. There are many upfront costs in concert promotion such as the rent for the venue. Some costs need to be paid at the end of the night such as the caterer, road crew, and even state taxes. All of these costs need to be resolved between the promoter and the artist. Who pays for what?

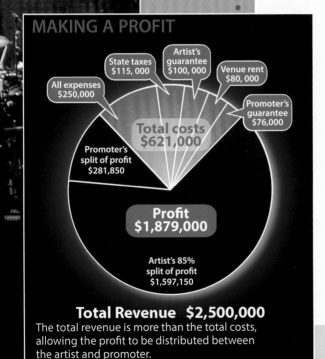

Linkin Park performs live during their A Thousand Suns World Tour on September 23, 2011, in Bangkok, Thailand.

## PROMOTER'S RESPONSIBILITY

The rent for the venue is one of the largest upfront costs a promoter has. Most large arenas cost an average of $80,000 for one night. Therefore, most concert promotions begin "in the red," which is a phrase used to express a profit loss or debt. The goal is to get your numbers "in the black" at the end of the concert. "In the black" means earning a profit or being **financially solvent**. "In the red" and "in the black" are phrases that go back to when accounting was done in a book with pen and paper. Red ink was used to show money owed, while black ink was used to show profit.

The promoter's production team and the artist's production team discuss all the requirements necessary, from labor to any types of audio, sound, and lighting. However, most artists these days travel with their own equipment. All expenses to do with dressing rooms and special requests, such as catering, are also discussed and agreed upon upfront. All of these expenses are put into what's called a rider, an upfront agreement managing the expectations of each leg of the world tour. Most of these items are, at first, paid for by the promoter but then settled, or paid back to the promoter, at the end of the night.

Then, when the box office totals the revenue from the concert, all the expenses are subtracted and paid to the promoter, venue, crews, and venue staff. After that, a profit split will be shared between the artist and the promoter. You will learn more about profit splitting later.

### MAKING A PROFIT

State taxes $115,000
Artist's guarantee $100,000
Venue rent $80,000
All expenses $250,000
Promoter's guarantee $76,000
Total costs $621,000
Promoter's split of profit $281,850
Profit $1,879,000
Artist's 85% split of profit $1,597,150

### Total Revenue $2,500,000

The total revenue is more than the total costs, allowing the profit to be distributed between the artist and promoter.

# ARTIST'S RESPONSIBILITY

## WARDROBE, TRAVEL, AND OTHER COSTS

The artist has costs associated with touring, too. He or she not only has to pay, but must also bear the expenses of their own travel and wardrobe. Also, at some point, most top performers will purchase their own lighting, sound, and other technical equipment.

Most artists on tour will have their own tour bus or plane. They will cover 100 percent of the cost to purchase these forms of transportation or they will rent transportation. They also cover all other travel expenses along the way such as hotel or housing rentals, food, and gas. Of the top performers, many will travel with their own personal chef. Jaime Laurita—also known as the Rock 'n' Roll Chef—has toured with bands such as Aerosmith, Madonna, The Rolling Stones,

## WHAT DO YOU THINK?

Which of these are expenses and which are income?
- venue hire
- security staff
- ticket sales
- decor/light show
- technicians and roadies
- parking sales
- merchandising sales
- food and accommodation for crew
- sale of TV broadcasting rights

Sting, Stone Temple Pilots, and the Red Hot Chili Peppers. These musicians feel that good food refuels them while on the road. Tours today can be grueling, lasting a year or more, including 100 or more shows, and spanning the globe. Comforts, such as a grand touring bus, fine food, and even a touring massage therapist, are necessary while doing such emotionally and physically demanding work.

## THE RECORD BREAKERS

Music listeners have streamed the equivalent of 1,500 years worth of music or 12,816,000 hours on Spotify alone, a digital-music service that gives access to millions of songs online.

"Beliebers" rush the tour bus of Canadian pop singer Justin Bieber in Stockholm, Sweden, on April 23, 2013. Bieber's Believe Tour was 15 months long with approximately 150 shows.

# TAKING A PROFIT

## THERE ARE NO GUARANTEES

You've probably heard the quote, "There are no guarantees," but in the music business there are two—the artist's **guarantee** and the promoter's guarantee. Remember, in the planning stages of the concert, the popularity of the artist was considered in order to choose the right venue. Another cost needed to be considered then, too. The artist's guarantee is the amount of money the artist is paid for the concert regardless of revenue generated or profit earned. The guarantee is **non-negotiable** for big names. Say you want to book Beyoncé. Before you can **project** your budget, you need to know her guarantee. The promoter also has a guarantee, usually less than the artist's. Once all costs are subtracted from the concert's revenue, the remaining profit is split—85 percent to the artist and 15 percent to the promoter. This is called profit splitting or profit sharing.

### INSIDER INSIGHT

"I grew up listening to Jay-Z, and I think the first time I really became obsessed with learning and thinking about lyrics was when I started listening to rap."
*Ezra Koenig, lead singer and guitarist of Vampire Weekend*

Glastonbury Festival contributes more than £100 ($163) million annually to the British economy.

## BACKING INTO THE BUDGET

Concert economics is a backward math puzzle. You start with the venue rent and guarantees, then work in your numbers. The venue holds 10,000 seats and the average cost of a ticket is $50. What is the **gross** profit before costs are subtracted?

Other costs:
Rent: $50,000
Artist's guarantee: $50,000
Promoter's guarantee: $40,000
Marketing: $75,000
Labor: $25,000
Production costs: $25,000

Subtracting these from the gross profit, what would it **yield** in pure profit?

## TOP 20 TOURING ARTISTS

### MILLIONS of DOLLARS

| Rank | Artist | Live Concerts | Recordings | Publishing | Total Income |
|------|--------|--------------|------------|------------|--------------|
| 1 | Paul McCartney | 64.9 | 2.2 | 2.2 | 72.1 |
| 2 | The Rolling Stones | 39.6 | 0.9 | 2.2 | 44.0 |
| 3 | Dave Matthews Band | 27.9 | 0.0 | 2.5 | 31.3 |
| 4 | Celine Dion | 22.4 | 3.1 | 0.9 | 31.1 |
| 5 | Eminem | 5.5 | 10.4 | 3.8 | 28.9 |
| 6 | Cher | 26.2 | 0.5 | 0.0 | 26.7 |
| 7 | Bruce Springsteen | 17.9 | 2.2 | 4.5 | 24.8 |
| 8 | Jay-Z | 0.7 | 12.7 | 0.7 | 22.7 |
| 9 | Ozzy Osbourne/the Osbournes | 3.8 | 0.2 | 0.5 | 22.5 |
| 10 | Elton John | 20.2 | 0.9 | 1.3 | 22.4 |
| 11 | The Eagles | 15.1 | 0.7 | 1.4 | 17.6 |
| 12 | Jimmy Buffett | 13.7 | 0.2 | 0.5 | 17.6 |
| 13 | Billy Joel | 16.0 | 0.0 | 1.0 | 17.0 |
| 14 | Neil Diamond | 16.5 | 0.0 | 0.3 | 16.8 |
| 15 | Aerosmith | 11.6 | 1.0 | 0.8 | 16.5 |
| 16 | Crosby, Stills, Nash & Young | 15.7 | 0.0 | 0.3 | 16.0 |
| 17 | Creed | 10.9 | 1.1 | 1.6 | 13.4 |
| 18 | Rush | 13.4 | 0.0 | 0.0 | 13.4 |
| 19 | Linkin Park | 1.7 | 4.7 | 6.3 | 13.1 |
| 20 | The Who | 12.6 | 0.0 | 0.0 | 12.6 |

The total pre-tax gross income earned by 20 selected touring artists. (rounded figures)

# 4 TICKETS AND PRICING

Once the stage layout is determined, the promoter, artist's manager, and venue owners walk the arena, deciding which seats cannot be sold due to obstructed views and which seats will be sold as **VIP** seating (the highest priced, closest-to-the-stage seats). From this, a seating manifest, or plan, is created and tickets go on sale. But how do they decide how much to charge? And why do tickets sell out so quickly?

Fans wait to hear American pop diva Lady Gaga in Singapore in 2012. Faced with the recession back home, more Western musicians are lured to Asia where **disposable income** is common.

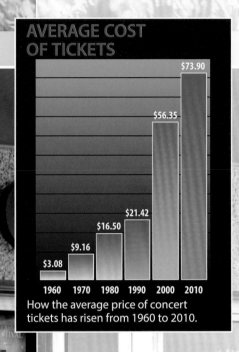

## AVERAGE COST OF TICKETS

| | | | | | |
|---|---|---|---|---|---|
| $3.08 | $9.16 | $16.50 | $21.42 | $56.35 | $73.90 |
| 1960 | 1970 | 1980 | 1990 | 2000 | 2010 |

How the average price of concert tickets has risen from 1960 to 2010.

### INSIDER INSIGHT

In 1980, you could buy a ticket to see Bruce Springsteen for $9.50. In 2012, the average ticket price for a Bruce concert was $92.68, plus fees.

*"Over the past four decades, two hours of live music moved from the entertainment column of the family budget to the category of major purchase."*
**Rick Chase, journalist**

## CHA-CHING!

Here's how promoters calculate what to charge for tickets: They consider the cost of the venue, the artist's guarantee, projected costs, and the projected revenue. Then they price the tickets accordingly to offset those overall costs. Supply and demand of the tickets come into play, too. If it's a high-profile artist who rarely tours, then those tickets will be in high demand, allowing them to charge BIG ticket prices.

Since you can't guarantee a sell-out, VIP packages are created to secure additional money. These packages offer the best seats in the house, an artist meet-and-greet, a photo opportunity with the artist, an autograph, and usually merchandise. Depending on the artist, VIP seats can cost anywhere from $500 for Maroon 5 to $2,000 for Justin Timberlake. Other more important artists who rarely tour, such as former Beatle Paul McCartney, could sell VIP passes for as much as $5,000.

## SOLD OUT ALREADY?

Tickets are not only sold to fans. They are also sold to radio stations, credit card companies, and other corporations. These tickets are then given away in promotions, to the artist's fan club to win in contests, and to the band's family and friends. As a result, a number of tickets are unavailable for sale to the general public.

So, the next time you hear that a venue has 15,000 seats, you'll know that fewer tickets are available for sale to consumers like you. In fact, between the band's family and friends and give-aways, maybe only 2,000 out of the 15,000 seats are left for purchase. The hotter the show and the bigger and more popular the artist, the less likely you are to grab any tickets for the concert.

# PRICE DISCRIMINATION

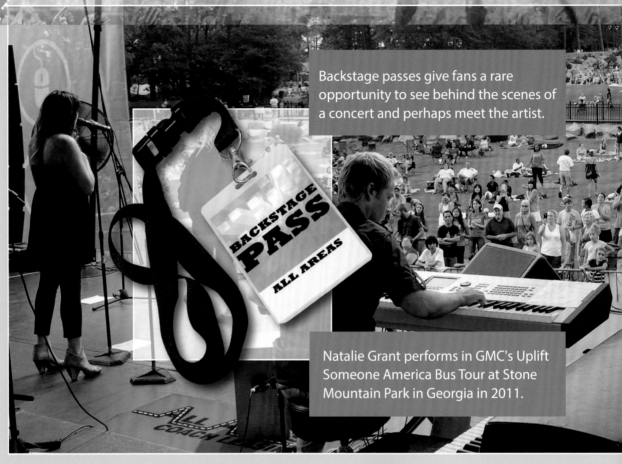

Backstage passes give fans a rare opportunity to see behind the scenes of a concert and perhaps meet the artist.

Natalie Grant performs in GMC's Uplift Someone America Bus Tour at Stone Mountain Park in Georgia in 2011.

## FOR THE PROMOTER

In the music business, **price discrimination** is a way of offering a variety of **price points** to fans with different **incomes**. One reason for staggering prices is to protect the promoter's investment in the cost of the venue.

Obviously, the promoter's goal is to earn a profit. While it's true that higher-priced seats yield greater revenue, a promoter could not sell out a concert if all 15,000 seats were set at the highest VIP price. If you charged everyone $2,000 a seat, your focus would be narrow, only attracting those with the most disposable income (money left over after necessities, such as rent, food, and clothing, have been paid). Think of it like a beam of light in the dark when you want to see as much as possible.

## THE RECORD BREAKERS

*According to research by editor Marlow Stern, Vampire Weekend was the most traveled band in 2010, covering approx. 150,000 miles (241,400 km). That's a little more than half the distance to travel from Earth to the Moon!*

## STADIUM SEATING PRICES

| Section | Lowest | Highest |
|---|---|---|
| PINK UPPER LEVEL SEATING (NOSE BLEED) | $73 | $806 |
| BLUE MAIN LEVEL SEATING | $115 | $884 |
| PURPLE MEZZANINE SEATING | $120 | $862 |
| RED HALL OF FAME SEATING | $144 | $880 |
| GREEN FIELD SEATING | $167 | $1,139 |
| YELLOW PIT SEATING | $3,400 | $3,400 |
| TURQUOISE SUITE SEATS | $9,400 | $14,900 |

The price of tickets for the Taylor Swift concert held on May 25, 2013, at the Cowboys Stadium in Texas.

If your beam of light is narrow, you can only see a sliver. But if you open your lens so that the beam is wide, you can see much more. For promoters, price discrimination is widening the beam of light that is cast on the fan base.

## FOR THE FANS

Since you and your friends do not have the same **earning capacity** (or pocket money), you cannot all afford the same things. As you now know, the concert is the product in our example and is an experience good.

But is this product the same for everyone? Chances are it isn't. Those in the first row may be lucky enough to reach up and touch the lead singer. Should a fan in the back row pay the same price? Discrimination offers a balance in the price inequity of the venue's seating.

## WHAT DO YOU THINK?

How would the price of tickets be affected if fewer were given away to the band's family and friends or as giveaways? How does price discrimination help you as a consumer? How does it hurt you?

# BRANDING A BAND

## CREATING A BRAND

One way to ensure the success of an artist is to create a **brand**. Branding attracts a target audience (a specific group of people). It includes everything from the types of music the artists perform to the clothes they wear, the haircut they rock, and whether they use heavy black eyeliner and black nail polish or have a more clean-cut image.

Managers and agents work very hard creating an image for the musician to target a specific gender, age, and/or **income bracket**. Everything is carefully calculated with this target audience in mind.

Compare, for example, the fans of Justin Bieber to the fans of Muse. Are they the same target audience? Justin Bieber's fans tend to be girls between the ages of 10 and 15. Muse tends to have more male fans than female, ranging in age between 15 and 30.

## BRAND EXTENSIONS

Once an artist has been branded, it's time to create other revenue streams (a way to make money). One way is through brand extensions, which is taking a product known for a specific feature and creating a spinoff product that is closely related to the original to create more sales to the same target audience. For example, in the food industry, one such brand extension is Arm & Hammer baking soda toothpaste from Arm & Hammer baking soda.

In terms of a musician's brand extensions while on tour, this would be concert T-shirts, posters, concert programs, and accessories with the band's logo on them. But brand extensions can continue outside the realm of touring. Many musicians have their own perfume and/or beverage lines. These are brand extensions.

### WHAT DO YOU THINK?

Let's get creative! Create a band. Give it a name and a brand image. Describe your target audience and think of some possible brand extensions.

### THE RECORD BREAKERS

In 2010, about 80,000 people attended the Bonnaroo Festival in Manchester, Tennessee, and produced about 489 tons (444 metric tons) of waste and 130 tons (118 metric tons) of recycled waste. The average total amount spent by each attendee for the four days was $1,440. This expense included the cost of tickets, travel, hotel, food, drinks, and souvenirs.

The heavy metal band Death Maze performs live at the outdoor festival, Kulturnatta in Umeå, Sweden, on May 21, 2011.

Sales from merchandise, such as T-shirts and posters, offer additional revenue streams for artists.

# A WORD FROM OUR SPONSOR

## AFTER-PARTY SPONSORS

After a large concert, there is often a party referred to as an after-party. After-parties can be lavish and expensive, and are usually for the band and their entourage. Most of these after-parties are sponsored, meaning they are paid for by large companies. Sometimes, there are many **sponsors**, each paying for something specific. Sometimes there is only one sponsor, fronting the whole event. Some parties have been known to feature a bar made completely of carved ice, sponsored by a well-known drink company. Why would a company do such a thing for an artist?

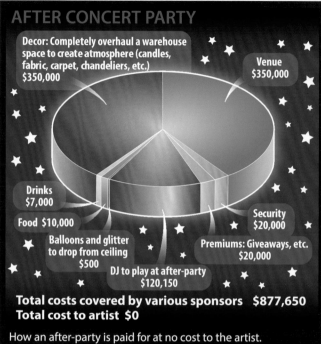

**AFTER CONCERT PARTY**

Decor: Completely overhaul a warehouse space to create atmosphere (candles, fabric, carpet, chandeliers, etc.) $350,000

Venue $350,000

Drinks $7,000

Food $10,000

Balloons and glitter to drop from ceiling $500

DJ to play at after-party $120,150

Premiums: Giveaways, etc. $20,000

Security $20,000

**Total costs covered by various sponsors  $877,650**
**Total cost to artist  $0**

How an after-party is paid for at no cost to the artist.

## ENDORSEMENTS

An endorsement is another type of sponsorship an artist can have. This type of sponsorship is not about lavish after-parties. With an endorsement, a company offers the musician a contract to be their spokesperson. This means the artist will appear in print and TV ads using their product. Often, musicians will sing the theme song for the product.

Successful endorsements relate to branding. If your musician is branded as an honest, sweet, clean-cut teen, then some possible sponsors to compliment his image may be soda companies. Sponsors mean big money for musicians. However, the musicians can't do anything to tarnish their image. Once they do, the endorsement ends. Sponsors are eager to throw money at big-name musicians in the hope that they will endorse their product. They want the public to see the band drinking their soda, driving their car, or wearing their sneakers. And if photographers capture a picture of a musician with their product, even better!

The audience enjoys Queen during a charity anti-AIDS concert on June 30, 2012, in Kyev, Ukraine.

# 5 THE BUDGET

Creating a careful budget is vital to your reputation as a promoter. You must consider every possible cost. Most crews are **union** employees. Union salaries and the cost of the venue are readily available information, so not much guesswork is needed. Experience and knowledge are a promoter's best friends. You are only as good as the accuracy of your estimated budget. That is basic economics.

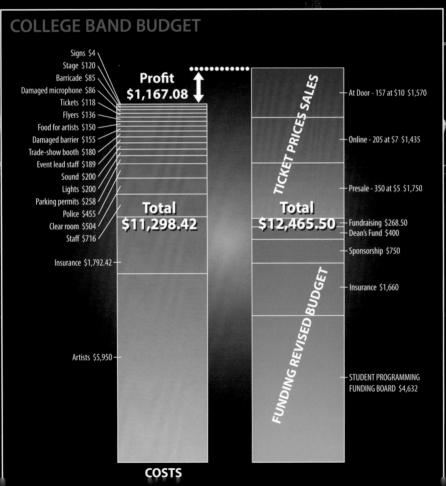

## COLLEGE BAND BUDGET

**COSTS**

Signs $4
Stage $120
Barricade $85
Damaged microphone $86
Tickets $118
Flyers $136
Food for artists $150
Damaged barrier $155
Trade-show booth $180
Event lead staff $189
Sound $200
Lights $200
Parking permits $258
Police $455
Clear room $504
Staff $716
Insurance $1,792.42
Artists $5,950

**Profit $1,167.08**

**Total $11,298.42**

**TICKET PRICES SALES**

At Door - 157 at $10  $1,570
Online - 205 at $7  $1,435
Presale - 350 at $5  $1,750

**Total $12,465.50**

**FUNDING REVISED BUDGET**

Fundraising $268.50
Dean's Fund $400
Sponsorship $750
Insurance $1,660
STUDENT PROGRAMMING FUNDING BOARD $4,632

## STAYING ON BUDGET

Someone on the promoter's team is responsible for making sure everything stays on budget. This person is the production manager. Production managers have a schedule of the day for all the crews. It is their job to make sure everyone stays right on schedule. A good production manager will always add into their budget overtime for union workers.

A typical day setting up for a concert could run like this:
8:00 A.M.–12:00 P.M.: Set-up, sound check, lighting, and special effects
12:00–1:00 P.M.: Lunchtime
1:00–6:00 P.M.: More setting-up, sound, lighting, special effects
6:00–8:00 P.M.: Dinner break
8:00–11:00 P.M.: Showtime!
If the show runs past 11:00 P.M., overtime fees start adding up. It's all about effective time management.

## SMALL-VENUE BUDGET

Remember price discrimination? A small venue cannot offer much variety in the way of seating prices because of its size. Most seats offer similar views and experiences. While a fan can expect some price discrimination, you see a much broader range with larger arenas. The challenge of a small venue for a promoter is having to ensure that most seats sell, because you won't have big-ticket VIP seats to offset losses on unsold seats. The advantage of a small venue is that it gives lesser-known bands the opportunity to increase their audience and test their market.

### WHAT DO YOU THINK?

List the five main skills that you think are absolutely necessary to be an effective production manager.

The Rapture performs at Razzmatazz in Barcelona, Spain, on November 22, 2011.

# LARGE-VENUE BUDGET

## LARGE-VENUE PROBLEMS

While large stadiums offer more opportunities for fans to grab tickets, they possess many potential problems for a promoter. First, big events are much more expensive to produce. Therefore, the financial risk a promoter takes by laying out the money upfront is far greater. Second, the sheer number of human resources needed to set up the concert is an immense operation. Usually, big venues mean very complicated stages. The bigger the operation, the more people involved, and the more likely problems will arise. It takes a team of people on the promoter's side, the artist's side, and the venue's side to make sure everything goes off without a hitch.

### TRICKS OF THE TRADE

On December 19, 2010, Muse performed at the Steel Blue Oval in Western Australia. With only one exit, it took hours for tens of thousands of fans to leave the outdoor arena.

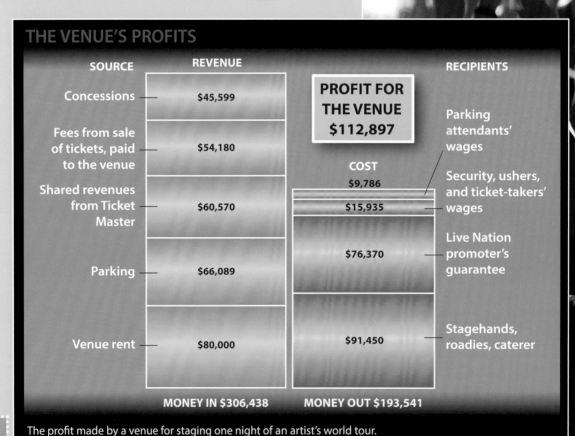

## THE VENUE'S PROFITS

| SOURCE | REVENUE | | RECIPIENTS |
|---|---|---|---|
| Concessions | $45,599 | | |
| Fees from sale of tickets, paid to the venue | $54,180 | **PROFIT FOR THE VENUE $112,897** | Parking attendants' wages |
| Shared revenues from Ticket Master | $60,570 | COST | Security, ushers, and ticket-takers' wages |
| | | $9,786 | |
| | | $15,935 | |
| Parking | $66,089 | $76,370 | Live Nation promoter's guarantee |
| Venue rent | $80,000 | $91,450 | Stagehands, roadies, caterer |
| **MONEY IN $306,438** | | **MONEY OUT $193,541** | |

The profit made by a venue for staging one night of an artist's world tour.

Crowd control is a serious issue at any concert—indoor, outdoor, large, or small.

## THE RECORD BREAKERS

Following 2009's No Line On The Horizon Tour, U2 embarked on their massive 360° Tour. The tour was a two-year global romp that brought in about $736 million in revenue—and nearly $200 million more than The Rolling Stones' A Bigger Bang Tour.

# THE THINGS UNSEEN

Bad weather can have huge effects on a concert budget. Heavy rain or snow can close a venue or prevent people from getting there on time.

## WEATHER PERMITTING

Even though a concert budget is pretty much a science, there is always the potential for unforeseen things to suddenly throw your budget off track. The biggest things to affect your budget are delays in setting-up, things that stop set-up, or shows running past 11 P.M. By far the biggest culprit of such delays is Mother Nature, of course!

Remember, most tours travel from country to country, state to state, and city to city. Plane or truck delays due to bad weather can mean you have crews sitting at the venue with no semi-trucks to unload. The clock is ticking, workers will be paid, but no work is getting done. There is nothing you can do but wait. Waiting can be frustrating as you watch your budget slip away.

## OTHER SETBACKS

Since most bands travel by bus, it is often very easy for someone to get sick. Due to the close-quarters of a tour bus, illnesses can spread rapidly from band member to band member. Most performers will push through illnesses that would put the rest of us straight to bed—but the show must go on. Canceling shows due to a performer's illness can have a serious impact on your budget. So when a show is canceled, it usually happens for a very good reason.

Rarely, injuries can occur for crew members or fans. If the crowd control is not well-maintained, resulting injuries can lead to lawsuits. Such lawsuits can be an enormous drain on a budget. Many promoters, agents, and artists take out **insurance** to cover the cost of any problems.

## TEN HIGHEST-GROSSING TOURS OF 2012

| | | Total Gross ($ millions) | Total attendance | Number of shows |
|---|---|---|---|---|
| 1 | MADONNA | 228.4 | 1,635,176 | 72 |
| 2 | BRUCE SPRINGSTEEN & THE E STREET BAND | 199.4 | 2,165,925 | 72 |
| 3 | ROGER WATERS | 186.5 | 1,680,042 | 72 |
| 4 | MICHAEL JACKSON THE IMMORTAL WORLD TOUR (by Cirque Du Soleil) | 147.3 | 1,374,482 | 183 |
| 5 | COLDPLAY | 147.3 | 1,811,787 | 67 |
| 6 | LADY GAGA | 124.9 | 1,111,099 | 65 |
| 7 | KENNY CHESNEY & TIM McGRAW | 96.5 | 1,085,382 | 23 |
| 8 | VAN HALEN | 54.4 | 522,296 | 46 |
| 9 | JAY-Z & KANYE WEST | 47 | 371,777 | 31 |
| 10 | ANDRÉ RIEU | 46.8 | 490,165 | 99 |

Who grossed what in 2012, and how many people saw them.

### WHAT DO YOU THINK?

According to the table above, the top three highest-grossing tours of 2012 were musicians who have a wide appeal with an adult target audience. Using what you now know about economics, what do you think is the reason these mostly adult crowds resulted in the highest-grossing tours?

# 6 ROCKING ON

Promoters don't only look for huge sell-out tours. They also keep their ear to the ground hoping to discover the next new talent. There is no such thing as an overnight success. Musicians spend years and years—maybe even most of their lives—sharpening their acts. And then, something happens. Some connection clicks into place. After all that hard work, a tipping point occurs to take them to that next level. What—or who—tips the scales in their favor?

According to an American survey conducted in 2012, nearly 49.2 percent of teens spend $0 a month on music, because they download it for free; 54 percent have a music app on their smartphone; and 64 percent listen to music through YouTube. Some teens do all three.

## YOU ARE IN CONTROL

Teens create today's music trends. Consumers have the power to determine what products or goods will be produced. This is called consumer sovereignty. In terms of the music business, consumer sovereignty occurs by simply clicking "like" on social media sites such as YouTube. Consumers decide which videos go viral. Before a musician can even grab a pen to sign on with an agent, she (or he) can go from singing alone in her bedroom to 5,000,000 hits in a few days. Today, it takes one hit song to propel the artist to that next level. Social networking sites put the consumer directly in the driver's seat of the music business. With the click of the thumbs-up button, they cast a vote sealing the fate of a song and its artist.

## WARP SPEED AHEAD

Justin Bieber, Cody Simpson, Soulja Boy, Walk Off The Earth, and Colbie Caillat—what do these people have in common? They were all discovered on the Internet. There is no doubt about it: The Internet sets a career path for warp speed. In the 1960s, bands grew their reputations slowly, one record at a time. Fans had a long-term relationship with their favorite musicians. However, with the quick road to success for some of today's musicians, they can find themselves unprepared to deal with their "overnight success." Therefore, having a strong team of managers, agents, and promoters can be vital to the longevity of their career.

## THE HIGHEST-GROSSING U.S. TOURS IN 2011

1. U2: $293,281,487; 44 shows
2. Bon Jovi: $192,947,951; 68 shows
3. Take That: $185,175,360; 29 shows
4. Roger Waters: $149,904,965; 92 shows
5. Taylor Swift: $97,368,416; 89 shows
6. Kenny Chesney: $84,576,917; 55 shows
7. Usher: $74,954,681; 73 shows
8. Lady Gaga: $71,900,434; 45 shows
9. André Rieu: $67,104,756; 102 shows
10. Sade $53,178,550; 59 shows

# LOOKING TO THE FUTURE

## INDUSTRY PREDICTIONS

Artist manager Jeff Rabhan, in his article "Music Industry Predictions: Labels, Concerts, Licensing and More," predicted a future for music that is already coming true. He believes the hard-ticket stub is on its way out the door to join up with vinyl records and the Sony Walkman. Most people purchase, or buy, tickets online. Rabhan believes that soon concert-goers will simply swipe their smartphones for entrance into a concert. Some experts predict smaller, more personal venues will become the next thing. At higher prices, they can offer fans a more intimate experience listening to their favorite bands perform live.

## STREAMING VERSUS LIVE

Although nothing beats the live experience, sometimes a concert is too far away or expensive, making a fan's ability to see it live impossible. What's the next best thing to experiencing a concert live? Seeing it

## INSIDER INSIGHT

"Ever since I was younger, I wanted to be on stage, singing my songs in a glittering costume. And that happened and is still happening. I have to remember that this is what I wished for and be grateful."
*Katy Perry, singer*

stream live in your living room, snuggled under your blankets. Let the other fans brave the rain, parking problems, and the soaring prices of tickets, food, drinks, and merchandise, while you watch from the comfort of your own home.

Festivals such as Coachella and Lollapalooza have already begun to stream live for fans who, for whatever reason, cannot make the gig. Do you think one day live concerts will disappear completely? If you hope not, remember this: By buying a ticket, you cast your vote to ensure the concert business stays alive and kicking.

## WHAT DO YOU THINK?

Turn back to the figures on page 41. For each artist, divide the gross earnings by the number of shows performed to calculate the average gross earned for each show. Now reorder the artists. Are they in different order? How does taking the number of shows into consideration affect the order?

## THE RECORD BREAKERS

According to Live Nation, in 2009, live music was the second-most-popular form of entertainment: about 52.1 million people attended concerts that year, while 73.4 million people attended baseball games.

The future of the music business lies in YOUR hands!

# GLOSSARY

**brand** A name, symbol, or design that differentiates a product from other products

**budget** A financial plan that considers one's total income and expenses

**cash flow** A way to measure money coming in and going out

**commission** A varied income based on earning a percentage from the revenue generated, usually relating to sales

**consumer** A person who buys goods and services

**deflation** A decrease in the cost of goods

**disposable income** The amount of money left over after all living expenses have been paid

**distribution** Supplying products to businesses that sell them to consumers

**earning capacity** The amount of money one can potentially earn

**economics** The study of the manufacture, distribution, sale, and use of goods and services

**economy** The way a country manages its money and other resources to produce, buy, and sell its goods and services

**entrepreneur** Someone who comes up with an idea to create a business

**experience good** A product you pay for before knowing its quality

**financially solvent** Being able to meet financial obligations and pay debts

**fixed expenses** The expenses in your budget that do not change

**free market** An economy based on supply and demand with little or no government control

**gross** A company's revenue minus the cost of goods sold

**guarantee** The amount of money in a contract paid regardless of profit or loss

**human resources** People and the skills they possess to perform a task

**incomes** How much money people earn for the work they do or things they sell

**income bracket** People who have a similar income

**inflation** A rise in the cost of goods

**insurance** Financial protection against loss or other mishaps

**investment** The money an investor or promoter puts into a business

# GLOSSARY

**limited resources** The finite amount of money each of us has

**marketing** The advertising, delivery, and selling of a service or good by targeting a specific audience

**negative numbers** Figures that occur when a company owes more money than it makes in profit

**non-negotiable** Not up for discussion

**opportunity cost** Things you give up when making a choice

**price discrimination** A marketing strategy in which a company charges customers different prices for the same product

**price point** A range in price an individual can afford based on their limited resources and income

**production** Making and providing goods and services for people to buy

**profit** The amount of money that a company makes after all the costs of running the business have been paid

**project** To forward-plan a budget by predicting costs and revenue

**recession** A period of high unemployment and failing businesses; the opposite of "growth"

**recoup** To regain, through profits, money that was spent or lost

**revenue stream** A niche or gap in the market where a company can make money

**scarcity** When there are not enough goods and services to satisfy the wants and needs of the consumer

**sponsors** People or companies who wish to be associated with an event by investing money

**supply and demand** A basic economic theory in which the demand (wants) of the consumer drives the supply (production) of a product

**trade-off** The choice made to give up one thing to afford another, due to the fact that their resources (money) are limited

**union** An organization created to represent the collective interests of a particular group of skilled laborers

**varied expenses** The monthly expenses in a budget that change from month to month such as groceries, transportation, and electricity

**VIP** Very Important Person

**yield** Income returned on an investment

# FIND OUT MORE

## BOOKS TO READ

**Acton, Johnny, and David Goldblatt.** *Eyewitness Books: Economy.* Dorling Kindersley, 2010.

**Andrews, Carolyn**. *What Are Goods and Services?* (Economics in Action). Crabtree Publishing, 2008.

**Challen, Paul.** *What Is Supply and Demand?* (Economics in Action). Crabtree Publishing, 2010.

**Flatt, Lizann.** *The Economics of the Super Bowl* (Economics of Entertainment). Crabtree Publishing, 2013.

**Girard Golomb, Kristen.** *Economics and You, Grades 5–8.* Mark Twain Media, 2012.

**Hollander, Barbara.** *Money Matters: An Introduction to Economics.* Heinemann Raintree, 2010.

**Hulick, Kathryn.** *The Economics of a Video Game* (Economics of Entertainment). Crabtree Publishing, 2013.

**Johnson, Robin.** *The Economics of Making a Movie* (Economics of Entertainment). Crabtree Publishing, 2013.

## WEBSITES

**http://dailyinfographic.com**
Information of all types presented visually

**www.billboard.com**
Facts, figures, and news about the music industry

**www.scholastic.com/browse/collection.jsp?id=455**
Articles and activities about the economy

**www.socialstudiesforkids.com/subjects/economics.htm**
An overview of economics

**www.the-numbers.com**
Box office data and records

# INDEX

# REFERENCES

## ACKNOWLEDGMENTS

The author wishes to thank the following people for assistance and credit these sources of information:

## Books

Flynn, Sean, Ph.D. *Economics for Dummies.* Hoboken: Wiley Publishing, Inc., 2nd Edition, 2011.

Klein, Grady, and Yoram Bauman, Ph.D. *The Cartoon Introduction to Economics: Volume One: Microeconomics.* New York: D & M Publishers, Inc., 2010.

Larson, Jennifer S. *Who's Buying? Who's Selling?: Understanding Consumers and Producers.* Minneapolis: Lerner Publishing, Inc., 2010.

Larson, Jennifer S. *What Can You Do with Money?: Earning, Spending, and Saving.* Minneapolis: Lerner Publishing, Inc., 2010.

Waddell, Ray D., Rich Barnet, and Jake Berry. *This Business of Concert Promotion and Touring: A Practical Guide to Creating, Selling, Organizing, and Staging Concerts.* Crown Publishing Group, 2007.

Wolfe, Leonard. *Easy Economics: A Visual Guide to What You Need to Know.* Hoboken: John Wiley & Sons, Inc., 2012.

## Websites

www.socialstudiesforkids.com/subjects/economicsbasic.htm

http://kids.usa.gov/money

www.vrml.k12.la.us/cc/economics/economics.htm

## Industry Reports and Articles

"Aerosmith Concert... Behind the Scenes," *Today Show,* 2004.

"Average Ticket Prices," Pollstar, 2013.

Chace, Zoe. "How Much Does It Cost To Make A Hit Song?" Planet Money, June 30, 2011.

"The Concert-Tour Economy," *Newsweek,* June 5, 2011.

*Economics Vocabulary,* Teacher Created Resources, Inc.

Etu. "Economist Alan Krueger examines pricing of concert tickets," News at Princeton, September 24, 2002.

Firecloud, Johnny. "Top 10 Highest Grossing Tours of All Time," Crave Online, August 9, 2012.

Krueger, Alan B. *The Economics of Real Superstars: The Market for Rock Concerts in the Material World,* April 12, 2004.

Plummer, Robert. "Winners take all in rockonomics," *BBC News,* April 20, 2006.

Rabhan, Jeff. "Music Industry Predictions: Labels, Concerts, Licensing and More," Reverbnation, January 31, 2013.

Tanners, Jon. "Fascinating Music Industry Stats," Pigeons and Planes, December 7, 2012.

"10 Interesting Facts about the World's Most Famous Arena," USA Student Travel, April, 20, 2011.

Vie, Ryo. "The Price Of A Concert: Breaking Down Where The Money Goes," The Rock and Roll Guru, March 20, 2011.